PAUSE

Reflect • Evolve • Design
Your New Lifestyle and New You Now!

PAUSE

Reflect ● Evolve ● Design
Your New Lifestyle and New You Now!

Christine Trainer

PAUSE: Reflect Evolve Design
Your New Lifestyle and New You Now!

Copyright © 2015 by Christine Trainer

For information, contact Christine Trainer at
www.REDIntegrativehealthcoach.com.

Disclaimer

The content of this book is for general instruction only. Each person's physical, emotional, and spiritual condition is unique. The instruction in this book is not intended to replace or interrupt the reader's relationship with a physician or other professionals. Please consult your doctor or health care practitioner for matters pertaining to your specific health and diet.

ISBN 13: 978-0692399705

Printed in the United States of America.

Contents

Dedication i

Acknowledgments iii

Foreword v

1 Life Happens 1

2 Which Way Is Up? Sound Familiar? 7

3 Break the Cycle and Trust Your Gut! 13

4 Time to PAUSE 21

5 What Works for YOU? 35

6 Nourish 41

7 Press Start, NOW! 47

8 RED Habits 57

9 Grace Mantras 61

10 Convenient Healthy Shopping 63

11 RED Easy Healthy Recipes 71

Conclusion 91

Thank You 93

About the Author 95

Resources 97

Dedication

This book is dedicated to
my husband, John, and
our amazing little men, Jack "JT" and Alec.

You have opened up a world to me, and
I am forever in love with and grateful for each of you.

For all my family and friends on this earth and in the heavens, I value each of you and our unique and individual relationships as treasures in my heart. You are a part of me and a part of this book. I thank you all and thank God for the continued blessings in my life.

Acknowledgments

I am deeply thankful to all the inspirational people in my life. I am blessed to have many!

A special thank you to my editor, Joni Wilson. Your expertise and professionalism made the process of polishing this book a pleasure.

To my girlfriends, I am forever grateful for your edits, your advice, your opinions, your time and sharing. I admire and respect you each and your help with input to this book has been invaluable, as your friendships are.

My four sisters, my five brothers, my in-laws and seventeen nieces and nephews. Your support, love and belief in me inspires, challenges and has pushed me to make this dream a reality.

My mom and my dad in heaven and my brothers, Al and Matty. You are with me always and part of this book.

Most important, I want to express my love and gratitude to my husband, John. Your patient support throughout this process and our deep love carries me.

Finally, thank you to my two sons, Jack "JT" and Alec, for whom I want to learn that anything is possible. Never stop going after your dreams and always keep loving.

Foreword

Go ahead and jump in! Read with your heart wide open and be ready for some self-exploration along the way.

"Everyone has a doctor in him or her;
we just have to help it in its work.
The natural healing force within each one of us
is the greatest force in getting well."

—Hippocrates

1

Life Happens

CONSIDER THAT IMAGE of a hamster running on a wheel—running in circles over and over again but never getting anywhere. Sound familiar? That was me.

I was your typical twenty-something. I was a young professional excelling in my marketing career. Although I was not passionate about my job, I liked playing the game—and I was good at it! I never said no to anyone. I never skipped an opportunity to attend an event, whether business or social. I was the first to volunteer for everything. I was the hamster on the wheel.

I was born in Boston, Massachusetts, Christine Grace O'Sullivan, the youngest of 10 children in the family. I was surrounded by hard-working, smart and talented individuals who I was (and still am) proud to call my family. They inspired me to try to do my best in all my pursuits. While my family followed a work hard–play hard mentality, I sometimes forgot about the playing part. Nonetheless, I was lucky to have had a happy, healthy, loving childhood with good values, religion, exercise and hard work instilled in me from day one. A born people pleaser, I always tried to be a great student, a well-behaved daughter, a good sister and a good friend.

I went to a small, private high school, where I received great grades and was well-liked. I excelled in college and was planning on law school. I ended up graduating with a double major in finance and marketing. As much as I was good with numbers, I loved the personal aspect and psychology involved in marketing.

After college, I started marketing consumer products in the adult beverage industry. I was a rising star at the company. My employer was supportive of my plans to go to law school. All was going according to plan.

Just three months after college graduation, my boyfriend of seven years was stabbed to death by a stranger. My world was shattered. What just happened? Losing Matt was life altering for me. I did not go on to further my education, but rather threw myself into work and the grind. I was 22 years old.

It was during this sad time that my love for running was born. As healthy and healing as the running was for me, I was truly running away from my mind, feelings and reality. I clearly remember my father saying to me, during this period of my life, "You can fool the rest of the world, but you can never fool yourself." Listening to his words and looking at myself was too painful; so I just worked harder, ran longer and dug deeper. I experienced night sweats and would wake with clenched fists.

Two years later, time was slowing healing me. At work, I started talking to this great guy, John. After some time, he asked me for a date. It had been tough for me to be happy in

Boston and unimaginable for me to go on a date—but I did. We began spending more and more time together, and, as much as I tried to resist, I fell in love again.

John was presented with a career opportunity that would take him to the District of Columbia. I took a leap of faith, got a great job for myself and moved to DC.

The move to DC could have been daunting for anyone, but it was especially difficult for someone like me—the youngest of 10 children and after all that happened when we lost Matt; however, it was, at the time, the best decision for me. The move gave me freedom from some sad memories and engrained expectations (most of which I placed on myself). The move enabled me to reenter the world with a fresh beginning and start living for me.

It was during this move to DC, when I started cooking and practicing yoga. My new reality was being true to who I really was—being true to the real me and what I aspired to be in my life. I let go of any feelings of who I should be, what I thought my life was going to be like and just let myself BE. I read about cooking, lifestyle, diets and travel. Most important, I was deeply in love.

John and I got married in July 2001 and both took jobs back in New York. Life was good. I was in a corner office on Fifth Avenue. I became completely submerged in my marketing, promotions and advertising world. It was a fast and fun time, but I lost myself again to the frenetic routines.

Three months later, in October 2001, my mom was diagnosed with Alzheimer's. Dad and our tight-knit family did all we could to stall our mother's deterioration from this horrible disease. John was incredibly supportive. John and I drove to Boston almost every weekend for the first five years of our marriage. He knew that my mother and I had a special and close relationship. I wanted every moment with her that I could get. I desperately imported Memantine from Canada. This drug, which was not approved by the US Food and Drug Administration (FDA) at the time, was supposed to slow the process of the disease. It did slow the progression for her a bit and, thankfully, we were still able to enjoy some time together.

I worried every day that I would get a call that something had happened to my mom. I got that call, but it was not about her. On May 5, 2004, at 4AM, I received a call that my second oldest brother, Al, had died suddenly after an insulin attack. Al had been a juvenile diabetic since age 11, and he was only 48 when he passed. I was devastated. What just happened? Again? Al's death rocked my family and my world. Al was this incredible, calming presence to be around. He was an amazing dad and loving husband, brother, son and friend. I still miss him; we all do.

When I gave birth to my first son, John Trainer III, "Jack," the following September, my father (the man who was told by his doctors that he was "strong as an ox") was just not himself anymore after losing Al. My father, who never took a pill, did daily push-ups and sit-ups and read and wrote constantly, was now a shadow of himself. Four months later in deep grief and heartbreak, my father was in pain, had lost weight, and was inactive and short of breath.

In October 2004, he was diagnosed with mesothelioma from exposure to asbestos. He had 50 percent lung capacity and was told there was nothing that could be done. He died on January 3, 2005. Seven months later, my mom passed.

When each of my parents died, my brothers, sisters and I were surrounding them, holding hands as they passed on. There was strength in numbers as we held one another up—but there was still such sadness. My family had changed so much, so drastically, in such a brief amount of time.

During this painful time, I went back to being "super me." While grieving about the deaths of my brother, Al, my dad and my mom, I was working as hard as I could—both personally and professionally. I still felt like I had to do everything, all the time. No matter how hard I tried to balance my life, my Type-A personality sabotaged not only my calendar, but also blocked my ability to shut down work, be present with my family and get some sleep.

Losing loved ones at such a young age made me want to live life more fully and make the most of each day; but instead, I ended up running on fumes, hurting my body, not living in the moment and not being present. Although I did not realize this at the time, I never gave myself a chance to take a breath and, therefore, never took the time, in my heart, to inventory what I really wanted to do. The race kept me from taking notice of how I was feeling about ME and how I wanted to feel. I was stuck in the race and was always thinking about its next leg, rather than taking that breath.

In 2007, I began developing chronic autoimmune diseases (which I will discuss later in this book). Why was this happening to me? I was young, fit and healthy. So many things outside my control had already happened to me in my life. Well, as you will see, this turned out to be within my control and, ironically, the best thing that could have happened to me, because it made me actually stop and look at my life. I was forced to PAUSE.

▲

Why am I writing this story? Why am I telling you about all the loss in my life? It is because I truly believe that our health is a statement of the condition of our minds, our hearts and our guts. It is not just about what food you feed your body or your genetics. It is about you and the balance in all areas of your life. This book is about getting the most out of life, feeling good and being healthy on the inside and the outside.

I hope to help you get there. Whether you are dealing with chronic autoimmune disorders or just not feeling good in your skin, there is hope—and you deserve it. How about a happier, healthier, sexier, glowing, more chic you? It starts with a PAUSE.

2

Which Way Is Up? Sound Familiar?

WAKING UP AT 5 AM to run on the treadmill, after a night of breastfeeding the baby and reassuring a toddler after a nightmare, was not the ideal mindset to begin a workout; but I did it because I was on autopilot. The nanny was arriving at 7 AM, and I had to make the train to my office in the city, which didn't allow much time to sleep in or catch a workout later.

I would arrive at my office—on time, of course; but not first without a daily stop at Starbucks for my first of three to four venti, white-chocolate mochas of the day. Yes, I said it— fairly disgusting. Sometimes I would even start out with two, just because. This was a daily routine and continued for the first four-and-a-half years of my first son Jack's life. There were breaks when I lost my brother, my dad and my mom, seven months apart. There was also a break when I gave birth to my second son, Alec, and was home for maternity leave for 11 weeks. Other than that, my schedule was unrelenting and grabbing sugar to infuse false energy along the way was standard. Autopilot . . .

At my desk, I got right to work with meetings, conference calls and reports, all while in the back of my head wishing I had taken the time for a healthy breakfast. I would think of my boys and how I had rushed out in the morning. It was only 9AM, and I wanted to take back the day. Despite those thoughts, I would quickly get lost in my scheduled workday. It was a dynamic office and industry; however, I did not love or believe in what I was doing. I simply loved the competitive game, and I was good at it. I would work through lunch, unless entertaining clients or being entertained. I ate only what I could pick up at Starbucks with my second or third cup of coffee and snacked on boxes of candy. I loved my Hot Tamales!

Calls came in, and I would be finishing a project or caught in a meeting until the last working minute. Every day I ran to catch my train home; however, the day never really ended at 6PM. On the train, I would try to complete my work and plan for the next day, so I would be able to be present with my boys when I got home. I would walk through the door at 7:30, or later, and pick up where the nanny left off with dinner, baths and bedtime. All I wanted was a few more hours just to be able to play and BE with my boys and my husband, John. This was the routine—the cycle that was my life.

▲

As I mentioned, I truly believe that our health is a direct reflection of our states of mind, our hearts, and our guts. Heartbreak, grief, and chronic stress all play into our body functions, and do damage that might result in disease and death. Autoimmune conditions and diseases that I have personally endured, and that are far too common in our culture, are a result of the stressors and the toxins surrounding us in our modern autopilot environment. It is inflammation in one form or another and is rampant in our culture.

Common autoimmune conditions are: alopecia, anemia, hepatitis, dermatomyositis, diabetes (type 1), some forms of juvenile idiopathic arthritis, Graves' disease, Guillain-Barré syndrome, Hashimoto's thyroiditis, inflammatory bowel disease (IBD), some forms of myocarditis, multiple sclerosis, psoriasis, rheumatoid arthritis, scleroderma, Sjögren's syndrome, lupus and Wegener's. Whether you or a loved one have an autoimmune condition or Alzheimer's—believe it or not—it's inflammation. There are no genetic sentences predisposing someone to these immune conditions. It all stems from our guts. To be healthy and feel good, we need to start with our guts.

Even though I was working, traveling, and a nanny was taking care of John's and my sons, I was still attempting to be healthy and at this point was eating only organic food. I breastfed our son until he was two; but, our pantry was still full of processed foods. I was still drinking about four Starbucks lattes or white mochas a day, along with boxes of candy and dried fruit and nuts. I was running during any free moments I could, while away on business at a hotel or if I was at home. I had gotten away from yoga and meditation and was on autopilot again.

I had a miscarriage (at 14 weeks) in December 2005 and then, in April 2007, had my second son, Alec. Alec was a happy, healthy baby, until he was about three months old, when he started having reflux. I was told it might be dairy foods in my breast milk. I stopped dairy, but at six months, he started getting ear infections. My other son had not had one ear infection and now my second son had nine ear infections between six and twelve months old. This was new territory for John and me.

We were scared as young parents and, in desperation, we finally agreed with our doctor to get tubes put in Alec's ears. The ear infections went away after the tubes were implanted, but ear infections turned into bronchial infections. Alec had pneumonia twice, and we were told he had chronic bronchitis and restrictive airway disease. It was just one antibiotic after another, and my beautiful boy kept getting sick. We could not go anywhere without a nebulizer and a bag full of prescriptions. I struggled with why my son had so many ailments, when we were living in what, I thought, was a healthy lifestyle.

In June 2007, I was not feeling right and thought it had to be more than just being a tired mom. I was diagnosed with Hashimoto's disease and hypothyroidism. I had been diagnosed with Raynaud's phenomenon eight years earlier. That diagnosis got me started researching inflammation and chronic illness. While I understood the reasons for these conditions, I still could not believe this was happening. All sorts of medications were prescribed. What was happening to me??? I was young, active, a runner and, I thought, I was healthy.

I started taking the thyroid prescription but could not bring myself to take the others, as I really could not think of taking them for the rest of my life. I was struggling, working and traveling so much. I was missing my sons and my husband. John and I decided we needed a change. John got another great job offer and instead of saying no, as I had in past (because I was "too invested in my career," even though not fulfilled), I said yes.

It was a welcome and needed change and a move to Chicago would be a clean break for me and my Type-A personality. As much as I wanted to be with my children, I did not want to have to give up my career. Thankfully, I finally began to see the decision not as sacrificing what I wanted, but, rather, I saw it as an opportunity that life was offering to me—to us, our family.

My father's words from years before came back to me, and I was ready to face them.

> *"You can fool the rest of the world,*
> *but you can never fool yourself."*

It was Dad's words and the story of my life that made me realize that I was finally ready to look in the mirror, accept responsibility, let go of excuses, so that I could reach for true happiness and fulfillment.

What is your story? Is your life just "happening"? Take five minutes, right now, and write some of your thoughts, on the following page, of where you are in your life and how that might differ from your childhood dreams or the story you wanted to live.

Notes.

3

Break the Cycle and Trust Your Gut!

SO I MOVED to Chicago. Here I was, Christine Trainer, a suburban stay-at-home mom. My new title and new workplace took some accustoming. I was ready for it. I opened my mind and, more important, my heart for this new chapter in MY story.

Naively, I thought I was going to have all the time in the world to be a mother, super wife, healthy cook and community volunteer while figuring out my next career plan. This was to be the life balance I was looking for. I believed that this new phase would be easy—just a sweet, fun, no-stress home life. I WAS WRONG! I kept telling myself that this phase in my life was short term and, that once I figured out how to balance, I would find my next career.

As I jumped with both feet submerged in the community and all the activities for my sons and our family, I was starting to realize that, although I was happy, something was missing. I believed, foolishly, that it was my career that I was missing. I believed I was biding my time until I could figure out what my new career was going to be. Then it hit me. My new career had to be **me**! I knew I had to work on finding and getting back to me. Since I was always thinking about what I was supposed to be doing next, I did not know who I was. I had drifted so far from myself that I knew I had to start the important work on myself. While I did not how I was going to "find myself" (sounds cliché, I know); I knew and felt that I had to start.

During this transition, I was still drinking my four Starbucks a day, downing candy like water and running on fumes. Working out, whether in my basement gym, running outside pushing my double jogger 3–7 miles a day or hitting the gym for a boot-camp class, I really thought this was how to be healthy. I would "balance" my bad habits by eating tons of fresh veggies and drinking gallons of water; but those bad habits were undermining the good ones. The damage might not have been outwardly visible; but, I was experiencing pain, throbbing in my joints, swelling of my knuckles, bloating, dry skin, brain fog and digestive disorders.

My blood work continued to show the hypothyroidism and the Hashimoto's, and the Raynaud's and continued to worsen. I was now also showing deficiencies in vitamins B and D. My new doctor told me that I had lupus. I remember thinking *there is no way.* I had just run a marathon and felt great. I remember leaving the doctor's office wondering, *Am I doing this to myself?* That was the day that I chose to make a change. It was my time to PAUSE and restart.

Where to restart? The answer had been with me my whole life—it was my gut! I learned that roughly 60–70 percent of our immune systems are located in our guts as a vast network of lymph tissues, called "GALT," or gut associated lymphatic tissue. Most common irritants that cause inflammation of GALT are sugar, gluten, soy and dairy.

Those ingredients were in my daily diet—in EXCESS. Never did I think I was an addict; but now, as I look back at the extent I ate candy and drank Starbucks, I realize that I truly was a sugar addict.

Growing up on low-fat, fat-free, alternative processed food had given me the taste for sugar. Sugar is actually eight times more addicting then heroin, and our processed foods are loaded with it—without any warning label. As I continued in my adult life, living the dream on the typical American diet, the amount of sugar in my seemingly healthy diet was outrageous. I knew I had to reverse years of bad eating. Enough was enough. I had been a believer in all the myths about fat; but now I started educating myself and my family about whole foods and a clean lifestyle.

I finally stopped to really think about what I was eating and feeding my family. Although I was not eating at fast-food joints, I was a major consumer of processed foods, which are nutrient depleted. Our fast-paced culture leads so many of us (including me) to the path of convenience; that is, programming us to buy into the foods on the go phenomena. Processed and ready-to-eat foods are everywhere, not just at fast-food joints. Fast-cooking, microwave meals that are prepared and ready to just heat and eat are a major part of the standard American diet.

I was part of that culture; but, as I started to eat clean, whole foods, I began to notice my aches and pains lessening, my fogginess clearing, my energy and stamina increasing and all of my senses reawakening. Instead of stocking my pantry with food that had a "shelf life," I was shopping more often for fewer items and simply focusing more on fresh, whole, perishable foods. Perishable is actual a positive term when it comes to food.

As I said, this was my time to PAUSE and restart my new me and my new lifestyle. That's just what I did! I took control and realized how I wanted to live. I realized the type of life John and I wanted for our family. We went for it.

Alec continued to be sick, and we were told he had allergy-induced asthma. He was prescribed an inhaler and a daily pill. I was uncomfortable and was not willing to accept this regimen for our son. While not a life-threatening illness, the thought of giving our baby pills every day scared me. I wanted an alternative for Alec. I didn't feel inhaled steroids for our sweet little boy was the answer.

We started a garden; cooking healthy, homemade meals; juicing; making smoothies and only eating organic. We got a lot of fresh air and exercise. Alec was improving. I was still on a prescription for my hypothyroidism and hated having to take it every day, but, was not sure how I could stop. I started doing yoga again and was training to run another marathon. In the back of my mind, however, I was still feeling like I wanted to do more. I was still feeling the urge to do more in this life—but this time it was going to be different.

The "more in my life" was going to be something I loved and something about which I was passionate. I had always been inspired by helping others. At this point, I realized that I could help others by telling my story and teaching them how to be happier, healthier and more fulfilled. I knew I had to figure out a way to make that my new mission and career.

Turning 40 made me realize the time to figure this out is now. My research started. I wanted balance in my life and for others.

"Follow your passion. The rest will attend to itself.
If I can do it, anybody can do it. It's possible.
And it's your turn. So go for it. It's never too late to
become what you always wanted to be in the first place."

—J. Michael Straczynski

I am following my passion and if I can do it, so can you. It's your turn, and I hope I can help.

My passion led me to become a certified holistic integrative health coach at the Institute for Integrative Nutrition™ in New York City. I established RED Integrative Health Coaching. Reflect, Evolve and Design Your New You Now, it all starts with a PAUSE.

> **Reflect**: Reflect on where you are in life, how you feel and the relationships in your life.
>
> **Evolve**: Look at the way you choose to spend your time. This can be an awakening and lead you to the evolution of yourself.
>
> **Design**: Let go of what does not serve you; accept the true you and design who you want to be and how you want to live.
>
> **RED** is a continuous process and should never stop for any of us. We are incredibly complex beings, and the world around us is constantly changing. Therefore, we need to constantly reflect, evolve and design.

As I devoted myself to this vision I started talking to my doctor about stopping my thyroid medication. She helped me lower the dose and get my vitamin B and D deficiencies under control by recommending that I completely eliminate gluten, soy and sugar. I did just that. Slowly my caffeine and sugar cravings lessened. I went back to her every three months and got my blood tested. I continued to lower my dose until I was able to stop taking it all together.

When the holidays came, I had gluten and sugar at a party. I had a horrible reaction. I thought it was because I was off my thyroid prescription and went back to the doctor feeling terrible; but my blood work actually came back with normal thyroid levels, along with normal vitamin B and D levels. It was simply a gluten reaction. Once my body rid itself of the gluten and sugar, I was fine—even better than fine, because I no longer needed my prescription medicine. After being told I would need it for the rest of my life, I found myself off the prescription. Alec and I were both now finally medication free! It was possible for us, and it is possible for you!

Are you in a cycle of taking prescription medications, battling autoimmune conditions or just feeling sluggish? Don't you want to break that cycle? Trust YOUR gut. Take a minute to reflect and write any thoughts, on the following page, that come to mind.

Notes.

4

Time to PAUSE

TAKE A PAUSE. Let yourself check in and assess where you are in life, where you are heading and where you want to be. While the past, in some ways, shapes who you are, you cannot let previous negative experiences define you. Instead, I encourage you to defy any previous negativity and try to be who you are meant to be.

> *"Life is 10% of what happens to you and 90% of how you react to it."*

—Charles R. Swindoll

These are powerful words. I often repeat these words to my children and to myself. We are faced with choices every moment of every day, assuming we are present and are listening to our hearts. Remember the old saying, "No need to cry over spilt milk." It is so true. While I have heard this saying millions of times, I still, as a parent, have gotten frustrated about a little mistake, even though I tell my children not to overreact. It's those times that I am not looking in the mirror. I need and you need to be mindful enough of our thoughts and actions to really let them become part of our own life guidelines.

We might not have control over what happens to us in life; however, we do have control over how we react. Own your moments, and do not let frustration, anger and guilt take over. So whether you have to excuse yourself, breathe and count to 10, or just slow down and think before you act or speak on emotion, allow yourself to do so. It is empowering when you can practice this in your daily life.

One of my dear friends was a foster child, in the system until she was four-and-a-half years old. She experienced severe abuse and neglect. She was lucky enough to be adopted into a wonderful, loving family and has lived a fabulous and blessed life since. If you ask her about her past, she will tell you the story and be bluntly honest; but, she will also make sure you understand that she does not let her negative beginning define her. She holds herself and who she is today accountable for her life, her actions, her failures (albeit few, if any) and her many successes. She is a prime example of a woman who did not let her past define her present. While you might not have had the childhood, the marriage or the job that you would have wanted, or life might have been "unfair" to you, how you react, and not the thing to which are you are reacting, defines you.

Do you choose to take responsibility, or do you blame? Do you choose to be positive and overcome setbacks, or do you wallow? Not taking responsibility can hold you back, because there is energy lost to blaming something or someone. Let it go, own it. We all know how awful we feel when we lose our patience or let a frustration get the best of us. Take time now to reflect on how you can start to own each moment. Write some notes, or just think about them and let them be.

I discuss the importance of our "Primary Food™" and balance of "Primary Food" with my clients. "Primary Food" consists of our relationships, spirituality, career and exercise and self-care. If we are out of balance in these areas, then our health can be negatively impacted. In other words, it's not just the foods we eat that affect our health.

In fact, that which we put into our mouths is "Secondary Food." We can be eating the healthiest diet, but if our Primary Food is not balanced, we can end up holding weight in our belly. We might not be able to lose those last 5–10 pounds. Sleeping poorly or experiencing chronic infections are all due to an imbalanced Primary Food intake. Our Primary Food is literally the key to our well-being. Many people look to a diet as food-based, but a Primary Food diet has nothing to do with food we put in our mouths.

In my work, I help clients find balance in these areas of Primary Food; however, what might help one person might not help another. That is because Primary Food differs from person to person, and everyone's diet and body chemistry is different. I have found, however, that no matter what the diet is, success in feeling great and being healthy is **first** based on balancing our Primary Food.

Relationships

Let's start with relationships. Whether you are single, married, a single parent or co-parent, friend, child, sibling, or cousin, everyone has relationships in their lives. If you do not or are feeling lonely, then you need to reach out. Human connection and love is the first priority.

My mom, as a mother of 10 kids, was a relationship guru in my eyes. She was constantly saying "let it go"; "forgive and forget"; and "I love you." Her hugs were meaningful moments that, for me, stopped time from moving. Her mindfulness (a term we hear more often these days) and loving ways kept our family close, even with 10 kids with differences as individuals.

Our lives are filled with many different relationships—family, friends, partners, spouses, etc. We need to look at our relationships and how they feed us. Are they healthy? Are they balanced? How do I feel when I am with this person? Not all relationships are meant to survive for a variety of reasons. We need to look deeply at ourselves to find if we are truly happy in our relationships. Often times, there is miscommunication, a lasting hurt or an unresolved resentment.

Regardless, if we hold on to these negatives in our lives—in our hearts—they become toxic. Until you let go—whether it's the hurt or even the relationship itself—your life will suffer. I suggest writing a letter as a step forward in the process of forgiveness or a step toward simply letting go and moving on.

There are many compelling studies about how love and nurturing are fundamental, basic human needs. Try starting today with taking a PAUSE from your busy day to connect with at least one of your relationships. Start or end your day with a hug. Hugs are therapeutic. Look into the eyes of your loved one, if you can, and be present with them. Take the time to make the phone call, FaceTime, meet at a café, or go for a walk together—see how you feel afterward.

Two treasures born from my newfound love of meditation and journaling are: (1) to make a conscious decision every day to be a positive force to those around me; and (2) to make a connection every day with someone outside my immediate family—whether a neighbor, a clerk at a store or bank, a person at the gym, etc.

It is a positive energy connection that is healthy and healing for them—and for me! Life goes by way too quickly; we are moving fast and always planning our next thing. If we are not careful, we will wish it away and our relationships along with it. Take time for those in your life.

Spirituality

Now, let's talk about another Primary Food, spirituality. Just as I believe food and diet are considered Bio-individuality™, a concept I will detail later, so is spirituality. Whatever your "religion," get in touch with your spirituality. In fact, one of the theories on the origin of the word "religion" is that it can be traced back to the Latin word "religare" which means "to tie" or "to bind."

Knowing that we are all "tied" to a greater purpose, a greater strength and greater meaning is so powerful and important. You see? Religion does not necessarily mean being part of an organized church (although it can mean that for some— and that's great!). If you are not affiliated with a particular religious group, then, consider a yoga practice or meditation. Yoga and meditation, along with journaling can be deeply spiritual. Give yourself the time to practice and find or deepen your spirituality. Let this start your day and remain with you throughout each day.

We hear a lot about mindfulness these days. I believe it is because of the frenetic design of our modern daily routines that people are getting lost in the various cycles of life and losing touch with spirituality. We need to be mindful and find stillness despite complex routines. It might not be easy to let go of the clutter inside our own minds; pausing and then listening to and trusting our senses is a first step.

It's just that easy—take five minutes where you can sit quietly and just let your senses take over. For those brief five minutes, forget the "to do" list and worries and just hear any sounds around you and allow yourself to feel any sensations. Then let that all go, and just be. Just be . . . Once you are able to get to that level of peace, savor it, then store it and carry it with you.

That inner peace, that mindfulness, will help you get through the mayhem that can occur around you in your daily life. Be aware of other beings around you and share that inner peace with them. Let it be your "go to" happy place. If you give yourself this gift, no matter how busy you are, you will find more time and be more productive then you would think.

It works. I am living proof. Think back to some of the stories from my life, which I shared with you earlier. Despite the intense sorrow and loss that I experienced (over and over again), I am as happy as I had hoped I'd ever be. I attribute that healing, that peace and that hope to the Primary Food I "eat"—and it all starts with pausing, being present and then just being.

Career

Next is career. Career is a difficult area for most to find balance and fulfillment but is a crucial Primary Food. How happy are you in your career? What is your life's purpose? Whether you are a professional or a stay-at-home mom, dad or a combination, do you find what you do for the majority of your time each day fulfilling? If yes, then fantastic and carry on. If not, then what can you do to make your time more fulfilling?

It might not always be a career change that is needed; but, rather, a shift in your approach, your mindset and your day. If it is a career change that is necessary to find true happiness and fulfillment, then what can you do to make that happen? What are you good at? What are your passions? What do you wish you had more time to do? Is there an opportunity in these answers? Prioritize and take steps toward what you want in your life. There is no time like the present and it is never too late! I promise.

Exercise and Self-Care

No matter what fitness level, we need to move every single day in order to be healthy. Period. If you are limited for time, try to take the stairs, park farther away from the door or walk or ride a bike instead of driving. If you can move a little every day and build up your strength, you will feel better and be happier. Do something—anything—to move, sweat; get your heart pumping and your lungs breathing deeply.

There is no one work out that is best for everyone, so try various routines and activities until something connects with you. It is out there and your body, your heart and your mind need it. Experiment and have fun with it. Do not give up after one try. Keep moving and you will feel better. Set goals and keep at it. Do not be critical of yourself but applaud your efforts.

Focus on the positive momentum increasing as you increase your fitness plan and feel great for it! Set-backs happen; but; the important thing is that you keep at it. This is your body—you only get one. Your body is the vehicle in which you travel throughout your life. As your body affects all aspects of your life, it's obviously best to feel good about it.

"If we could give every individual the right amount of nourishment and exercise, not too little and not too much, we would have found the safest way to health."

—Hippocrates

Self-care is a big part of balance in our lives and feeling good about ourselves. Taking time for ourselves might be the hardest thing for some people to do. We are often so defined by our career, our role as a parent or spouse, that our self care gets interrupted. Our "to do" list and many roles we play cause us to forget about taking time for ourselves.

Personal time to reflect and PAUSE, getting proper amounts of sleep, being present in our interactions, eating mindfully and consciously, taking time to chew and breathing deeply every day are key to our health and happiness. Sexuality also comes into play here and how we allow others to love us, as we love ourselves. The better we feel about ourselves and the more in touch we are with our bodies, the more comfortable we are with our sexuality.

Stop being critical of yourself, forgive yourself and move on. How about trying to have unconditional love for yourself? Take a minute to think about that and write how you feel. We will revisit this issue again later in the chapter on Nourish.

Okay, so pausing and looking inward at ourselves might not always be easy, but give yourself the opportunity to do just that. Take PAUSE and think about your Primary Foods. Are you working on fostering healthy relationships? Even now I need to check in every day with myself and see how I am feeding ME. Making sure we are nourished with our Primary Foods is key to our overall well-being.

If you find that you are not balanced, think about what you can do each day to improve your Primary Food balance. Do not beat yourself up about it. Make a list of intentions. Prioritize and start making small changes each day, so that you can feel balanced in these areas. Start acting on your intentions. You can do this!

With all things in life, time is of the essence. No matter the age, in our modern culture we are all feeling strapped for time. Even children complain about being stressed out nowadays. Look at your life and your time. What do you spend your time doing every day? Think about the things that suck the life out of you, and try to fill that time with positive things that fill you up.

Because you are now taking inventory and feeding yourself Primary Foods, think about what fills you up spiritually and physically. Focus on these foods. List the items, people, activities, duties, responsibilities and then prioritize. We have a mind-set of "more is better"; but, maybe as our world is changing and people are becoming more aware of our effect on the environment, on our food supply, on one another, just maybe we are realizing that LESS is more.

Prioritize your list of items and look for any non-Primary Foods that you might be able to cut out or cut back on. Take stock in your "diet." Make sure what's feeding you is what's fueling you in a positive way. Sometimes this is difficult to do. As a people pleaser, it is difficult for me; but, in order to be present for the priorities in my life, I have found that life is truly about quality and not quantity. Clarity guides me; let it guide you. You cannot be all things to all people.

Time management will help you prioritize yourself and balance your Primary Food. It is hard to manage when life throws so many curve balls in our schedules, work, family, kids, health, etc. Take time to PAUSE. It will allow you to look at everything in your life and reflect on your priorities. Reset, so that you can design your new life and your new you.

Have you heard about author/educator Stephen Covey's time management concept called Big Rocks? In his demonstration, he illustrates how we have one jar, which symbolizes our life. Then we have big rocks that symbolize our big goals and values. There are other sizes of pebbles that symbolize additional responsibilities and activities. Sand symbolizes the other miscellaneous "stuff" in our lives. If you put the big rocks in the jar first, all the other-size rocks and sand will fit, but if you put the small stuff in first, then the big rocks do not fit.

I help my clients to create their own jar of life and sort their rocks, big and small. It really brings to life that how you prioritize enables you to do more in less time. It also demonstrates that with focus and a "less is more" approach to life, you are more productive.

I work with clients on going through what their monthly/weekly goals are to help them organize by first identifying their top four to six goals and then filling in with other smaller goals and responsibilities. It is a great way to cut out what does not serve you and helps you to feel empowered to make the right choices. When you utilize your time most efficiently, it leads to your most fulfilling life.

You can start looking at your own time and activities and fill out the worksheet below. List your top three monthly and top three weekly big rocks, in addition to monthly and weekly smaller rocks. Then list any sand outside the chart below.

After going through the process of filling in the chart, reflect on how you spend your time now and how and if you are willing to change. Remember it is about quality and not quantity.

DATE			Total Hours
Top 3 Monthly Big Rocks	Top 3 Weekly Big Rocks	Monthly Smaller Rocks	Weekly Smaller Rocks

5

What Works for YOU?

ALL OF US have experienced a myriad of diets—whether personally or through family, friends, acquaintances, peers or colleagues. The cabbage-soup diet was one that was popular around the time of my wedding; then it was the South Beach Diet. Whether it's the no-carb diet, the low-carb diet, the Atkins diet, or the juice diet, these are not diets that take into consideration Primary Food.

Unfortunately, people tend to start these diets on a whim and it becomes a roller coaster for them and their bodies. Typically, these diets fail, not only because they are not sustainable, but also because no one diet is suited for everyone. This concept is called Bio-individuality.

We are unique individuals, with different blood types and different genetic and personality backgrounds from all over the world. Given these differences, it makes common sense that there is no one diet that suits everyone. That is why it is imperative to avoid diet trends and fads and look to yourself for what works for you.

You are an individual. You have it within yourself to know what is best for you. Connect with yourself, pay attention to your body and allow it to teach you what it needs. When we allow our bodies to figure out what works best on a Bio-individuality level, we can then adapt to what works for a lifetime—it becomes a lifestyle. Your "diet" needs to be a lifestyle change and a positive therapeutic experience. How great would it be to never go on a diet again?

Remember the phrase, "You are what you eat"? It is truer than you think. Our bodies actually evolve and renew from what we eat. Every 28 days, our skin replaces itself; every 5 months our liver replaces itself; and our bones every 10 years. The body renews by using the food we eat to produce new cells. You literally **do** become what you eat! Think of that concept and then think about everything you have put into and are putting into your body. Become aware of your body and take good care of it. It is your lab experiment, your temple and you need to respect it.

This concept of a lifestyle change should be (and can be) a positive, therapeutic experience. A lifestyle change does not deprive, but rather, it provides. I promise that you do not have to eat less or deprive yourself in order to eat healthy and achieve your weight loss and health goals. You can actually add food. Think about what you can add to each meal every day—what you can add to your life experience, your body and your temple. Maybe it is adding more vegetables to every meal and a salad every day or a green juice or all three.

Making those healthy choices first at every meal, every day, before eating other stuff, will help you crowd out the bad stuff. You will start to crave less and feel better. This idea of crowding out leaves the body and mind satisfied and full instead of feeling deprived and wanting more.

Making healthier food choices, eliminating processed foods and eating more food in its natural state is the key. The natural state of food allows our bodies to digest, metabolize and use the food to nourish our bodies and feel the best we possibly can.

What can you add to your daily eating habits? What do you want to eliminate? Remember to not deprive yourself. Be honest with your thoughts and write a few notes.

Starting a food journal is a great way to take note of what does and does not work for you. Stop feeling bad about what you ate; rather, document it. It will help you get in touch with your body more and your reaction to different foods. This will help you avoid what does not serve you without feeling deprived. There are some great food journal apps—I usually recommend the simpler, the better. Check out fooducate.com or another note app on your smart phone. You can also use a simple notebook and pen to record your food habits.

As you go through this process of finding out what works for you, water is incredibly important. Your body needs water—and a lot of it—every day. Start first thing in the morning by drinking water. After a night's sleep, your body is in a state of detox and is dehydrated. Nourish and rehydrate your cells with what it needs, living water!

Water will help your organs function properly and will allow your body to metabolize more efficiently. This will help the body rid itself of toxins naturally while quenching thirst. Depending on your activity level, you should increase your water intake.

A simple equation to ensure you are drinking enough water is to take your weight and divide by two. This is approximately what your body needs in ounces of water every day to stay hydrated. Again, if you are working out or sweating, then you need to increase that water intake level. Make sure you water yourself daily!

Fresh air does wonders for the mind, the body, the heart and the soul. Whenever you can, get out and breathe in some fresh air. Living in colder climates does not always allow for the relaxed walk outside; but brisk walking, parking farther away from doors and trying to get a little FRESH AIR each day is still beneficial and a mood booster.

We need to remember that in our daily lives, we need fresh air to open our lungs and oxygenate ourselves. I am not a cold-weather girl, to say the least, but I do try to get outside daily to breathe in the fresh, albeit cold, air. In warmer weather, I try to stay outside as much as possible. I can feel the difference when I am housebound and know when I need to get out and rock some fresh air.

Connect with your body, nourish it with what you need, empower yourself and get ready to THRIVE!

6

Nourish

We have all probably heard the phrase "unconditional love." This might be the love that exists between a parent and a child or the relationship between us and God. What about unconditional love for ourselves? We are too critical of ourselves, our bodies, skin, hair, features, and where we are at various points in our lives. Plastic surgeries are at an all-time high. Sad.

We have become a plastic society that might be smiling on the outside; but how many are feeling happy, loved and fulfilled inside their lives? There is more and more conflict in our culture and less and less love. How do we stop the cycle? How about starting with unconditional love for ourselves? We need to give ourselves the love, support and forgiveness to move forward and be the happy, healthy people we are meant to be. We need to be nourished.

Are you feeling nourished, or are you criticizing yourself? Do you have regrets? Whether you are off track, got frustrated with a spouse, lost patience with a child, please forgive yourself and move on. We do it with others in our lives; why is it so hard to give unconditional love to ourselves? It does not have to be difficult.

Once you allow your mind and heart to open to this new reality, you will feel relief. Go on, forgive yourself, be gentle, nourish yourself and be ready to move on and go forward. This might be a daily, weekly or monthly exercise for some— take the time you need, but keep at it. You deserve unconditional love for yourself in order to be the best YOU can be. Love yourself enough to truly change, and be the sexy, attractive, chic person you are.

Human connection is incredibly powerful. Taking time to connect and experience the world and people around us is what our souls need to flourish. When we think about nourishment, we think of the food that we put in our mouths. But going back to the concept of Primary Food, it is that "other food" that is the real true food of life. Relationships, love, spirituality, career or life purpose, exercise and movement are what we really need to be properly nourishing ourselves daily. Loneliness and negativity are toxic and more harmful to our bodies than anything we put in our mouths.

As rushed as we are, many times we waste the precious time we have by making hasty decisions. For example, not treating our loved ones thoughtfully, then having to go back and apologize and repair the damage. "Haste Makes Waste" was another one of my father's sayings. With having 10 kids, I guess he and my mom had seen plenty through their parenting. My parents found these types of sayings to be simple, but effective, teachings that did not have to be repeated over and over to get us to understand.

"Haste Makes Waste"—driving too fast and getting a speeding ticket; carrying too much in one bag and the bag breaks; being too quick to react and saying something in anger. The saying has always stuck in my head, more so regarding relationships and human interactions than anything else. I know that when I am moving too fast and not being present in conversations with my children or John, I feel empty and unfulfilled. I end up going back, looking them in the eye and really listening to what they need.

We are humans and need to connect, to hear and be heard by other human beings. Listen to the people in your life and let yourself be heard and understood. Being heard is necessary for release and healing. Human connection and positive relationships make for healthier, happier and longer lives.

There are many studies based on the connection between human relationships and longevity. One particular study was done in the 1966 with a group of people who came from Italy and settled in Roseto, Pennsylvania. In the study, this Italian-American community did not get heart disease or any other illnesses except from natural causes; whereas the people in the surrounding communities had incidences of heart and other diseases.

A team was brought in to study these people's habits, diets and lifestyle, as they hoped to find a cure for heart disease in our country. At this time, heart disease was at its height and prevention awareness was low. The study found that the people of Roseto were eating heavy foods cooked in fat, including pastas, meats, cheeses and breads. They drank wines and even smoked; yet they had half the rate of death by heart disease than the people from the surrounding communities.

The conclusion from the study was that the people had half the rate of death by heart disease because they were never lonely. The people of Roseto were living in a multi-generational community, that is, children, parents, grandparents, cousins were all living in the same community. They worked hard—the men worked in the rock quarry and the women in the blouse factory; but, they would come home and gather for meals. They all went to church together and they all helped one another—families and neighbors alike. This became known as the Roseto effect.

Loneliness leaves individuals feeling overwhelmed, helpless and puts the nervous system into stress response. That stress response, or "fight or flight" as Dr. Walter Canon from Harvard termed it, causes strain on our bodies, organs and causes damage over time.

The Roseto study continued and over time, as children were moving away from their families and the multi-generational, close-knit, Italian-American community began being dismantled, the people of Roseto began developing all the diseases, including heart disease, that were more prevalent in the surrounding communities. In 1971, the first heart attack death of a person younger than 45 occurred in Roseto. During the same period of time that American heart disease was declining, as education and awareness of a heart healthy diet and exercise increased nationally, the Rosetan's rate rose to the previous national average, as their close-knit community continued its deterioration.

So although that study had a sad ending, it clearly shows the impact that loneliness, close social networking and human connection have on our health. The more we get in touch with others and allow ourselves the time to truly connect with them, the healthier we can be. Allow yourself the time to connect and be present with those around you. It is good for you! This is not a mere luxury; rather, you should block time on your calendar (like you would an appointment or meeting) in order to make it a priority.

As we connect with ourselves and others, we will also start to get in touch with our intuition. We need to try to listen more to our intuition and less to our brains. Our brains are so mechanical and exposed to commercialism and modern culture, that getting back to our natural selves and listening to our intuition will help us make better choices in all aspects of our lives. I think I would have started doing this work many years ago if I had listened to and trusted my intuition. You can start trying now to nourish your intuition. You will find it easier to discern between your intuition and your ego the more you practice.

Be open. Organic opportunities come to us daily. Allowing ourselves to be open to what the universe invites, is vital to self-exploration and fulfillment. If we are not mindful of ourselves and present in our daily activities and connections, then we will miss these opportunities that are meant to be. Is it simply circumstance or synchronicity? What if it was your level of openness, your loving of yourself and simply being open to what is out there for you, that is holding you back from your life's purpose or your happiness and fulfillment?

Take time now, breathe deeply and think about how you feel you are truly nourishing yourself and your human connections. Grab a pen and write what you do now or what you can do to nourish. Start with daily; proceed to weekly, monthly and then yearly. It is a powerful exercise to help you see where there is an opportunity for you to be more present in your interactions.

7

Press Start, NOW!

DEVELOPING AND IMPLEMENTING a new lifestyle can sound daunting—I get it; but, you are merely doing what your body wants you to do. It's as simple as that. Connect with your body and empower yourself today by committing to be strong, healthy and happy. Honestly, the first step in approaching change is being open to making it happen for YOU. After that—it's all about choices—and the good ones are more fulfilling (on so many levels) than the bad ones. I promise.

> *"You must find the place inside yourself*
> *where nothing is impossible."*
>
> —Deepak Chopra

Life can be overwhelming. No matter who you are or at what point you are in your life, it might seem like you just can't win. I love the above quote by author and spiritual leader Deepak Chopra. He is basically saying that you just need to "dig deep" sometimes. The place inside yourself where nothing is impossible is there—you just need to find it and hold on to it.

Breathe and believe in yourself. Tell yourself that anything is possible, despite setbacks you might encounter, challenges you have to face or obstacles that you need to overcome. Nothing is impossible. A good way to start is to set small, measurable goals. Each and every time, feel accomplished with each goal you reach.

The small changes will have a domino effect. Small changes in your everyday choices will begin to add up, the culmination of which is a big change in your overall lifestyle and happiness. It's your new lifestyle, the one that you design and that did not just happen.

Choose the positive in every situation. It's amazing what happens when you do this. Smile and people will smile back, whether they meant to or not. It's a normal reaction that can spread. Try it. It really does work. Remember YOU are in control of the present moment and how YOU react to it—no one else. Don't let yourself lose focus on what you want to feel like and who you want to be.

Wake up on the right side each day and look for things about which to be thankful—whether it just might be the floor beneath your feet or a warming ray of sunshine. Gratefulness produces more thankful situations and opportunities.

Make a quick list of the things for which you are grateful.

Notes.

Now start your day—every day—by being thankful and thinking about your list. Add to it. Enjoy watching your list grow and deepen.

The harder choices might arise when it comes to food and health. It seems that when it comes to our health, we know what we should do; but the hardest thing in the world is to actually do it. Make the right choices for YOU and follow through. You are worth it and deserve it. You will feel better and see clearer about what your body needs to feel its best.

Again, start with small changes every day throughout the day. Rather than giving in to a sweet craving; give yourself some delicious, sweet fruit or a warm tea. It will become a routine and a lifestyle to the point that you will not be able to imagine another.

Food Choices

Satisfy your body needs; do not make food choices that won't stick. If you are craving something, think about why you are craving that particular food. Are you hungry, emotional, frustrated, stressed or did you not eat enough **good** food at your last meal? Plan ahead to help yourself make good choices on the go or to satisfy a craving.

For example have, on hand, a fruit salad in your fridge. Maybe cut up fresh veggies and snack with homemade hummus or guacamole. Make your healthy meals in larger quantities so you have healthy leftovers that you can heat up quickly as a meal, if you are in a hurry. Pack it for work the next day.

For example, have quinoa pilaf as a side dish one night, and then wrap it in a lettuce or cabbage leaf with some hummus for lunch the next day. That same quinoa pilaf can serve as a delicious warm breakfast porridge, if you add some almond milk, warm it, sprinkle it with cinnamon and vanilla and add a fruit of your choice (I like cut-up dates).

I will share with you some of my favorite go-to RED recipes later in this book; but, remember to make your food and eat your food with intention. Chew your food slowly and mindfully, and be thankful for it. Love yourself when you are preparing your food and when you are eating it. You want to be satisfied, fulfilled and in tune with your body. Being present and mindful when you are cooking and eating (especially healthy food) will leave you feeling fulfilled, accomplished and connected to your body.

Sleep Choices

Sleep and self-care are extremely important when it comes to your health and wellness. Please, don't skimp in these areas. As you are trying to be a super human being, do not do harm to your body by neglecting it or by burning the proverbial candle at both ends.

The average adult body requires anywhere from 7–10 hours of sleep, depending on the individual. This was, and still is, one area where I constantly struggle. It's amazing, however, that once I started really taking care of myself—getting more sleep, eliminating gluten and sugar, eating whole foods—my blood work started getting better. I now have normal thyroid levels and no longer have a lupus diagnosis!! Making changes, such as I did, becomes even more significant when there is a history of cancer, heart disease, Alzheimer's or autoimmune conditions in your family.

Not getting enough sleep can cause things such as premature aging, inability to lose weight, mood swings, lack of sex drive, memory loss, brain fog, serious illnesses (even more than the ones listed above) and strokes. Give yourself the sleep you need and try to be consistent about it.

If you have trouble sleeping, consider trying different therapies to help. A good first step would be to turn off electronics and let your mind relax for at least two hours before you try to go to sleep. Unplug and find stillness. Go for a walk, stretch, meditate, dim the lights, do not eat and be sure to let your body completely relax. Breathe—deeply and purposefully. Getting enough sleep reduces stress. Sleep also enables the body to repair itself, because the body goes through a rejuvenation process nightly while sleeping.

Letting Go Choices

Self-care also includes letting go of the negative. This is a huge step. Perhaps you should let go of any relationships that do not positively serve you. As difficult as that sounds, you deserve to surround yourself with people who fill you with joy, light, laughter and inspiration, and who challenge you to be the best you can be.

Be mindful of your feelings when you are spending time with someone. Do you feel depleted or anxious after a visit? Or are you invigorated and inspired? Pay attention and surround yourself with people who will love you and help you love yourself. Life is simply too brief. Love yourself enough to change and to let others love you fully.

Let go of the past, accept it and place your focus, energy, love and attention on the present. These things are necessary for peace in your heart and your mind. The present is truly the only thing over which you have control. Think about it—there is nothing you can do about yesterday and tomorrow isn't here yet. Own your present moment and be fulfilled by it.

A good way to let go is writing a letter that expresses your feelings. Whether it's mailed or not, this might bring closure to something that has kept you from finding peace and happiness. As human beings, we want to change our past and make it right. Simply put, you cannot.

The past is gone, and so must you go on. Wishing, wanting and wasting time on something over which you have no control can only become toxic over time—toxic to your body, your mind and your soul. When you let go, your relief will be great. Try it. No matter the level of letting go, when you truly do, you will feel it.

Take some time to write something about which you might want to let go. Forgive yourself or someone else and move on.

Notes.

Now I want you to write three small changes you can start to make. I am here to help you along the way. Reach out to REDIntegrativeHealthCoach@yahoo.com.

BE THE CHANGE YOU WANT TO SEE IN YOUR LIFE!

8

RED Habits

THIS IS A handy little chapter with some simple daily routines, quick tips, recipes and reference lists for shopping and becoming more in touch with your food and your new you.

I hope this is helpful—whether you are a juggling mom, a business traveler, in a corporate career or just want this as a go-to reference as you are on your journey to a healthier, happier life.

PAUSE

15 Daily Habits to
Restart, Reflect, Evolve and Design Your New YOU!

BREATHE deeply and slowly to start your day with intention. Journal and meditate, if you can. Find stillness in your life.

SMILE and let it brighten up your space wherever you are and feel the smiles come back to you.

OPEN your heart and mind to the day ahead.

FORGIVE yourself if you need to so you can move forward and forgive others so you can let go.

WATER yourself in the morning and continue throughout the day.

MOVE anyway you can to get your blood flowing. Get exercise into your day.

CONNECT with a loved one, give a hug or reach out to another human who needs it. Remember the power of human connection and nourish yourself in this area.

CHOOSE to be positive, to be accountable to your goals and to your intentions.

RAINBOW your plate—eating a rainbow of fresh produce will help you get all the nutrients your body needs.

CHEW your food and your thoughts.

Be **PRESENT** throughout the day to own your moments, being mindful and aware of your inner voice, your thoughts, your words, your actions and others around you.

LOVE yourself unconditionally and love one another.

Be **GRATEFUL,** as gratefulness begets more thankful situations.

Live with **GRACE** and practice grace.

Whatever your religion, take time to pray and be aware of the presence of **GOD** in the world around you.

9

Grace Mantras

JUST FOR FUN . . . I swear they work :)

I am _____ (your name).

I am enough.

I am loved.

I forgive myself.

I will be gentle with myself.

I will listen to my inner voice.

I will trust my heart.

I will follow my gut.

I will not let myself down.

I am worth it.

I will _____ (any thought or feeling that you need to voice, let it out).

My intention today is _____.

Today is a new day.

I am open to the abundance the universe is providing me.

I have hope.

I am light.

I am love.

Thank you, God.

PAUSE

10

Convenient Healthy Shopping

"Let food be thy medicine and medicine thy food."

—Hippocrates

TRY TO SUPPORT local organic farmers. It is the best way to ensure you are getting the freshest seasonal and most natural food, along with supporting local commerce and reducing your carbon footprint. Not only do you get all the fresh flavor and full vitamin benefit when eating local organic farmed produce, you also can experience new vegetables and meet the farmer and family who grows your produce. Famers' markets are a wonderful way to do this. Hit the next farmers' market in your area.

To find a great listing of farmers' markets, go to:
www.localharvest.org/farmers-markets/
or
www.usdalocalfooddirectories.com.

Join a community-supported agriculture (CSA), and even have fresh organic vegetables and fruit delivered directly from the local farm to your doorstep. LocalHarvest.com is a great starting place to look into joining a CSA, with the most comprehensive listing (along with reviews) in the United States. CSAs are not limited to produce and can include shares of eggs, poultry and beef, in some cases, if that interests you.

If you go to the grocery store and want to buy organic, but can't always afford to buy all organic, the next pages include easy, quick, reference lists to use.

RED
INTEGRATIVE HEALTH COACH
— Reflect, Evolve, Design Your New Lifestyle —

THE CLEAN FIFTEEN list of produce have the least pesticide contamination of conventionally grown crops. So if you can't buy all organic, this list helps you to save money, but still eat healthy.

- Avocado
- Sweet Corn
- Pineapples
- Cabbage
- Sweet Peas (frozen)
- Onions
- Asparagus
- Mangoes
- Papayas
- Kiwi
- Eggplant
- Grapefruit
- Cantaloupe

- Cauliflower
- Sweet Potatoes

THE DIRTY DOZEN has now turned into fourteen, with the last two of particular concern (blueberries and hot peppers) because of the highly toxic insecticides that are used in conventional farming of these crops. Always try to buy organic, if possible, the 14 items listed below. If you are traveling or do not have access, then you still need to eat vegetables, so take extreme care to wash them thoroughly.

- Apples
- Strawberries
- Grapes
- Celery
- Peaches
- Spinach
- Sweet Bell Peppers
- Nectarines (imported)
- Cucumbers
- Cherry Tomatoes
- Snap Peas
- Potatoes
- Hot Peppers
- Blueberries (domestic)

We all know it is overwhelming to read labels and understand what the fine print means. Take little steps in becoming more aware of what is in your food and being more conscious of what you are buying.

Here are two easy guidelines to follow when buying a packaged item.

First, look at it this way, if a product has a long shelf life, then it is not natural. It will have chemicals and preservatives in it that you do not want to consume.

Second, you definitely want to look for GMO free, which means genetically modified organisms, and you do not want those in your food and in your body for more obvious reasons.

Remember, you literally become what you eat, so don't put toxins in your body. Sometimes I work with clients on pantry makeovers and help them go through what they have in the house. Then I find alternatives for some go-to items that might not be serving them well.

Keep it simple and fresh, and try to keep to the fresh produce and refrigerated sections of your grocery store. Avoid going down those middle aisles, filled with packages of processed foods.

Build On Grocery List

Simplify a grocery list that you can use each time you shop. Save it on your phone or print paper copies. Build on to the list, depending on the recipes you are going to make. The following is my standard list that I build onto.

- milk (I use almond)
- eggs (pastured, organic, non GMO)
- greens
- veggies, to cut up for snacks
- veggies for recipes
- ginger
- garlic
- onion
- turmeric
- mint
- fruit for snacks
- lemons
- limes
- whole grains (gluten free pasta, quinoa, rice, millet)
- steel-cut oatmeal
- beans
- almond flour, for baking
- coconut palm sugar, for baking
- coconut oil, for cooking and for moisturizing
- olive oil
- raw almonds
- raw cashews
- sprouted pumpkin seeds
- sunflower seeds
- matcha green tea

Again, try to buy all organic and practice reading the labels of any packaged items you do buy. Remember: more than five ingredients or words that you do not know is a red flag to leave it on the shelf and walk away!

11

RED Easy Healthy Recipes

THESE ARE SOME great food and beverage ideas to help you avert the bad cravings and feel the best you can throughout the day and the week! I encourage you to try new recipes and introduce new food to your healthy diet. It's amazing what incredible food is available for us to nourish and strengthen our bodies, if we choose to embrace it!

Morning Beauty Elixir

Start your morning with a mug of warm water, lemon and a splash of apple cider vinegar. Or enjoy this as a cold drink. Enjoy the benefits.

▲

Daily H2O

Fill a carafe or a canister with fresh cold water and add your favorite fruits, along with some mint if you like, to sip on throughout the day.

Be creative and try new fruits and vegetables that sound interesting to you.

Here is a favorite concoction of mine:

Ingredients

- 1 cucumber
- 5 mint leaves
- 1 gallon of cold water

This is great to have handy and ready to sip on when we get a sweet craving or want seconds or thirds!

Green Goddess Smoothie

Ingredients

- 1 cup of fresh or frozen spinach
- 1 cup fresh or frozen kale
- 1 inch turmeric
- 1 inch ginger
- 5 fresh mint leaves
- 1/2 cup frozen mango
- 1/2 cup strawberries
- 1/2 cup ice
- 1/2 cup almond milk

The Green Goddess smoothie is a favorite of my husband and me. We add in a scoop of our vegan protein powder, a teaspoon of flaxseed, a teaspoon of chia seed and a teaspoon of maca powder, if we want it to be more filling and fueling.

Put all ingredients in a Vitamix or blender until it's a smooth consistency you like. Add water or more almond milk, depending on your preference.

Feel free to increase the greens and decrease the fruit as you get used to drinking green juice. It is packed with antioxidant super foods and has such a fresh, clean flavor, I feel like having another one now! Serves two.

Morning Hangover Cure Smoothie

We all overindulge at times so whether it was too much food or libations, this will help.

Ingredients

- 1 beet

- 1 cup dandelion greens

- 1 cup kale

- 1/2 cup frozen blueberries

- 1/2 cup frozen pineapple

Put all ingredients in a Vitamix or blender until it's a smooth consistency you like. Add water or almond milk, depending on your preference.

▲

Overnight Chia Pudding

This is great to have as an anytime snack or even a grab-and-go breakfast.

Ingredients

- 1/4 cup chia seeds
- 3/4 cup coconut milk
- 3/4 tsp cinnamon
- 3/4 tsp vanilla

Combine ingredients in a glass jar, mix and seal. Keep overnight in fridge, and then enjoy!

Overnight Oatmeal Parfait

This is a favorite breakfast of mine or an anytime snack.

Ingredients

> 1/2 cup steel or rolled oats (can split 1/4 c muesli or Ezekiel cereal with 1/4 c oats to mix it up)
>
> 1 tsp of currants
>
> sprinkle of cinnamon
>
> 4 ounces unsweetened almond milk
>
> 1 tsp of chia seeds
>
> 1 cup fresh or frozen fruit (my favorite is frozen blueberries)

Directions

In a "to go" glass container of your choice: Place oats, Ezekiel cereal/muesli, cinnamon, currants, chia seeds and almond milk in the container and stir. Top mixture with fresh or frozen fruit. Let mixture sit in fridge overnight or up to three days in fridge.

Serve cold right out of the fridge or warm in the oven for 10–15 minutes at 300 degrees.

Mini Frittata

Super easy and delicious. This is a great idea when you have overnight guests and want to be visiting in the morning with them and not flipping pancakes.

Ingredients

   4 whole eggs

   1 large red pepper, diced

   1 cup spinach fresh, or if frozen spinach drained of liquid

   ½ small red onion, diced

   1 to 2 ounces of munching or goat cheese (optional)

   3 tbsp minced fresh basil

   ¼ tsp red pepper flakes

   ¼ tsp paprika

   ¼ tsp sea salt

   fresh cracked black pepper to taste

   ½ tsp coconut oil (to coat muffin tin or use baking cups)

Instructions

Preheat oven to 375.Combine all ingredients in a large bowl.

Pour mixture into coconut oil-greased muffin pan.

Bake for 10 to 14 minutes or until golden on top.

Let rest for at least 5 minutes and serve.

Hummus

This simple recipe makes about 2 1/2 to 3 cups, depending on how smooth you make it. I make it about once a week to have with raw veggies when I feel like a snack. Add more spice to it or even top with an extra dash of hot sauce and a sprinkle of pine nuts. Make it your own!

Ingredients

- 4 garlic cloves

- 2 cups canned chickpeas, drained, liquid reserved

- 1 1/2 tsp kosher salt

- 1/3 cup tahini (sesame paste)

- 6 tbsp freshly squeezed lemon juice
  (2 lemons)

- 2 tbsp water or liquid from the chickpeas

- 8 dashes hot sauce

Directions

Put the garlic in the Vitamix or a food processor first to grind, then add the rest of the ingredients and blend until the hummus is pureed to the texture you want.

Feel free to add more chickpea liquid to further puree. Taste, for seasoning, and serve chilled or at room temperature.

Simple Quinoa

This healthy grain is great as a side dish, put into a lettuce wrap, fish taco or a burrito or sprinkled on top of salads. As a option you can quickly sauté some of your favorite veggies in oil or coconut oil and serve on top as a more filling side or even a meal.

Ingredients

   1 cup quinoa, rinsed

   2 cups of vegetable stock (or chicken broth or even simply water)

   1 tsp of salt in the water

Simply pour quinoa and liquid in small sauce pan and bring to a boil. Once boiled, reduce heat to a simmer and cover for 8–10 minutes until all liquid is absorbed.

Fluff with a fork and serve with sea salt and pepper and a squeeze of a lemon.

Asian Turkey Lettuce Wrap

Created by Dr. Junger's Clean Program | www.cleanprogram.com

Ingredients

- 1 pound ground turkey
- 2 tbsp coconut oil
- 2 carrots, finely chopped or grated
- 3 cloves garlic, minced
- 2 tbsp fresh ginger, peeled and grated
- 1 tsp Chinese 5-spice powder
- 2 tbsp wheat-free tamari
- 2 tbsp rice wine vinegar
- 1 tbsp coconut nectar
- 1 can water chestnuts, chopped
- 1 head Boston, Bibb lettuce or endive
- chopped cilantro
- 2 green onions, chopped

Directions

Melt coconut oil in a medium skillet over medium-high heat. Add carrots and sauté for several minutes. Add garlic, ginger, turkey and Chinese 5 spice to the pan and sauté until turkey is cooked through—about 3–5 minutes. Add water chestnuts and cook for three more minutes. Stir in tamari, vinegar and nectar. Cook for a couple more minutes, stirring well to thoroughly combine. Put one scoop of turkey mixture into lettuce leaves. Top with green onions and cilantro.

RED Quick Sauce

This sauce is simple, rustic and delicious and goes well with pasta, over quinoa, spaghetti squash, meatballs, chicken cutlets and even scrumptious with shrimp and pasta.

Ingredients

olive oil

1–2 heads garlic

small onion (optional)

2 cans of Italian whole peeled tomatoes
(add fresh plum tomatoes, if they are in season, instead of 1 can or just in addition to)

fresh parsley

fresh basil

sea salt

ground pepper

Cover bottom of stockpot or large sauté pan with olive oil. Simmer minced garlic until soft, add chopped onion, if you want, and cook until soft. Add tomatoes, two pinches of sea salt and ground pepper. Add 1/4 cup of water. Cover top of sauce with fresh chopped parsley and let boil down. Should boil 25 minutes, while you stir and mash tomatoes every 5 minutes. Turn heat to medium and add freshly chopped basil on top and cook to taste.

Baked Arancini

These quinoa/rice balls take 2–3 hours, but I make and freeze them to make the time worth it. They go great with my quick sauce.

Ingredients

- 1/2 cup walnuts, chopped
- 1/2 cup dehydrated porcini mushrooms, chopped
- 1 1/2 cup spinach, or defrosted frozen spinach, drained
- 1/2 cup parmesan cheese
- 1 egg, scrambled
- 3 cloves garlic, minced
- 1 small onion, diced
- 1/2 cup quinoa, rinsed
- 3/4 cup brown rice
- 1/2 cup Sauvignon Blanc wine
- 2 oz manchengo cheese, grated

Dice onion and garlic. In a medium pot on med-high heat, use the water method to cook the onions until translucent. (Water method is cooking the veggie on med-high heat and adding a couple tablespoons of water to remove browning from the pan.) Keep adding water until onions or veggies are caramelized. Each time, make sure to cook out the water before adding more veggies.

Next, add the garlic and cook for another minute. Add the rice, rinsed quinoa, pepper and salt to taste, white wine and water. Bring to a boil. Once boiling, reduce heat, cover and cook until all the liquid has been absorbed—about 40 minutes.

Add spinach, parmesan cheese, egg, chopped walnuts and chopped porcini mushrooms. Mix all the ingredients well. Transfer to a large bowl and place in fridge, about an hour, until completely cooled.

▲

Christine's Turkey Meatballs

This is my most requested meal from my sons and my husband to go along with my homemade red sauce.

Ingredients

1 pound ground turkey (lean 7% fat)

1 egg

gluten free breadcrumbs (if you can, try to find gluten-free flavored Italian breadcrumbs. If not, just mix in Italian seasoning. Or make homemade gluten-free breadcrumbs with Italian herbs mixed in)

Mix turkey and egg together in bowl. Then add just enough breadcrumbs so that the meatballs will not be watery—only about a 1/3 cup of bread crumbs. Mix well to get all the flavor into the turkey meat.

Bake at 350 for 30 minutes. Then put into the red sauce and cook, on low, at least another 30 minutes before serving.

Top It Salad

I love salads and love mixing it up with toppings, such as avocado, pine nuts, pumpkin seeds, sunflower seeds, quinoa or chopped walnuts. The following is my basic go-to salad that I just add any of the above ingredients to— whatever I feel like that day. It is really easy to have this in your fridge and be able to serve yourself and your family a nice salad that is balanced and delicious!

Ingredients

   1 package baby kale

   1 package baby romaine

   olive oil

   fig vinegar

   lemon

   sea salt

   pepper

For the dressing, simply mix 3 tbsp olive oil and 2 tbsp fig vinegar. Squeeze 1 tbsp fresh lemon and mix again.

Plate the baby kale and baby romaine. Layer with toppings that you have in your pantry and are wanting at that moment. Sea salt and pepper lightly and serve.

Homemade No-Bake Oatmeal Energy Bars

This is a simple, quick, clean snack to have on the go between activities or even as a fast breakfast, made the night before.

Ingredients

2 1/2 cups rolled or quick oats

1 cup raw pumpkin seeds (pepitas)

1/2 cup raisins

2/3 cup peanut butter or almond butter

1/2 agave nectar or brown rice syrup (adjust based on how well things stick together)

1/8 tsp sea salt (adjust based on which nut butter you use)

Mix oats, pumpkin seeds and raisins in a large bowl. Whisk together nut butter, sweetener and sea salt. Pour into oat mixture and mix well, until everything is sticky and combined. If it's too dry, add a bit more agave. Press mixture into a shallow baking dish that you've lined with foil or plastic wrap. Cover with more foil/plastic, press well into the baking dish, and refrigerate for 4 hours.

Cut into bar shapes, wrap, and keep refrigerated until ready to use. They will last up to two weeks in the fridge.

Raw Vegan Chocolate Fudge

Courtesy of Mav Kuhn of Mindful Holistic Healing

Decadent, delicious and to die for—if you like dark chocolate, then you are going to love this fudge.

Ingredients

   2 cups of dates (sugar-free, non-coated)

   1 cup of peanut butter (smooth, sugar-free)

   1 cup of solid coconut oil

   ¾ cup of raw CACAO powder
   (NOTE: this is CACAO powder NOT COCOA powder)

Instructions

1. Soak the dates in filtered water for about 4 hours. After 4 hours, drain the water.

2. Chop the dates finely in a food processor until it is as smooth a paste as possible.

3. Tip the date mixture into a large mixing bowl.

4. Add the peanut butter to the bowl.

5. Add the raw cacao powder to the bowl.

6. Heat the solid coconut oil in a saucepan until it is liquid and clear.

7. Add the hot, liquid coconut oil to the mixture in the bowl.

8. Mix vigorously all ingredients. It will seem watery and goopy at first, but it will eventually turn into a cohesive mixture.

9. Turn the mixture out onto a baking tray lined with baking paper.

10. Spread the mixture, so it is roughly ½ inch thick.

11. Place in the fridge. Leave for about 3 hours, before cutting into pieces and serving. Always store in the fridge to prevent the fudge from softening at room temperature (if allowed to soften, it will have more a consistency of a chocolate fudge brownie).

You can add other ingredients to flavor the fudge, such as pine nuts, hazelnuts, chopped Brazil nuts, stem ginger, raisins (avoid walnuts, unless you can get them blanched—likewise for almonds—as the skins are too bitter for the fudge). If you decide to add other ingredients, just add them to the mixture in the bowl, before you add the coconut oil, and then vigorously stir in.

▲

Christina's Cavewoman Bars

These bars are great to have around as a power snack, that sweet treat after a meal or a great dessert to share with friends and family. Enjoy!

Ingredients

1 cup slivered almonds

1 cup pecans

½ cup nut flour

½ cup unsweetened dried coconut

½ cup almond butter

½ cup coconut oil

¼ maple syrup, pure, not artificial

2 tsp pure vanilla paste

½ tsp salt

1 cup dried cherries or other dried fruit

Instructions

Preheat the oven to 350 degrees and toast the nuts until golden brown, stirring occasionally. Watch them carefully; they'll go from golden to black fast! Once they are toasted nicely, toss them in the food processor or blender and give them a few pulses until they are a coarse meal. Stir this into the nut flour in a medium bowl.

In a double boiler, warm the coconut oil and almond butter and stir them together well. Add the maple syrup, vanilla, and salt, and then mix until creamy. Fold the nut mix into the maple syrup mix, and then add the fruit. Pat into an 8 x 8 baking dish and refrigerate for at least an hour until solid. Cut into squares. Keep in the fridge to store.

Conclusion

MY HOPE IS that by sharing my story and the truths I have uncovered along my journey that you also might be inspired to make a shift in your life. Reference your notes that you made throughout the book, along with some of the easy reference pages I have included at the end of this book for convenient shopping, healthy recipes, RED daily habits and my favorite grace mantras.

I would love to work with you individually! I invite you to contact me at www.REDIntegrativehealthcoach.com.

It all starts with a PAUSE.

Thank You

Thank you for reading my book.

I would love to hear from you! Please post your review for this book at www.REDIntegrativeHealthCoach.com.

About the Author

CHRISTINE TRAINER is a certified, holistic, integrative health coach; inspirational speaker; marathoner; avid yogi; student and lover of life. Christine resides outside of Chicago, Illinois, with her husband, John, and two sons, Jack "JT" and Alec. She enjoys working with others through her private practice and finding balance and joy every day.

Resources

1. Stephen R. Covey, "The Big Rocks of Life," *First Things First* (Simon and Schuster, 1994).

2. "Institute for Integrative Nutrition," "Primary Food," and "Bio-individuality," are trademarks that are owned by Integrative Nutrition Inc. (used under license).

3. Alejandro Junger, Clean Program, www.cleanprogram.com.

4. Mav Kuhn, Mindful Holistic Healing, www.mindfulholistichealing.com.

Made in the USA
Lexington, KY
27 May 2015